D0597644

# THE CALIFORNIA GOLD RUSH

# THE CALIFORNIA GOLD RUSH

## WEST WITH THE FORTY-NINERS

BY
ELIZABETH VAN STEENWYK

FRANKLIN WATTS
New York • London • Toronto • Sydney
A First Book 1991

The quotes on pages 12, 14, 17, and 23 are from *Gold Dust*, by Donald Dale Jackson, published in 1980 by Alfred A. Knopf in New York.

Photographs courtesy of: Historical Pictures Service: pp. 2, 11, 13, 30, 34, 49; The Museums at Stony Brook, New York: p. 15 (Gift of Mr. & Mrs. Ward Melville); The Bettmann Archive: pp. 16, 26, 27, 37, 39, 40, 42, 45, 52; Museum of the City of New York: p. 21; Peabody Museum of Salem, Ma.: p. 25 (Mark Sexton); New York Public Library, Picture Collection: pp. 43, 47; Gamma-Liaison: p. 55 (Eric Sanders).

Library of Congress Cataloging-in-Publication Data

Van Steenwyk, Elizabeth.
The California gold rush : west with the Forty-Niners / by Elizabeth Van Steenwyk.
p. cm.—(A First book)
Includes bibliographical references and index.
Summary: Describes the 1849 California Gold Rush and life for the miners during and after the gold rush.
ISBN 0-531-20032-9
1. California—Gold discoveries—Juvenile literature. 2. California—History—1846–1850—Juvenile literature. 3. Gold mines and mining—California—History—19th century—Juvenile literature. [1. California—Gold discoveries. 2. California—History—1846–1850. 3. Gold mines and mining—California—History—19th century.] I. Title. II. Series.
F865.V28 1991
979.4′04—dc20 91-4672 CIP AC


Printed in the United States of America
6

# CONTENTS

# INTRODUCTION

**THE CALIFORNIA GOLD RUSH** was one of the most important events in nineteenth-century American history. With the exception of the Civil War, the gold rush caused more changes in Americans' lives than any other episode in the 1800s. It completed western expansion to the Pacific. It gave identity to the fledgling state of California. And it opened new routes of transportation as thousands migrated to the gold fields, where they hoped to make their dreams of riches come true.

In 1849, more than 50,000 men, as well as a few women, rushed to the hills and rivers of California when they heard gold had been discovered there. They were called "forty-niners," after the first year of the gold rush. Because they were so eager to get to the gold, they endured many hardships—illness, harsh living conditions, bad weather, and violent crime—to pursue their dreams.

The forty-niners were a restless group. They moved from one mining camp to another, always hoping to find bigger nuggets of gold or richer veins of ore over the next hill. When they did find gold, many couldn't hang on to it. They lost it in the gambling halls of the camps. Or they lost it to the high prices they were forced to pay for food and shelter.

The forty-niners soon realized that they could find more gold if they worked together. They used new methods to dig out hard-to-reach veins of ore. Working together meant smaller profits for each miner. For many, it simply wasn't enough on which to live.

Many miners left California and returned to the families they'd left behind. Others sent for their wives and children. They then settled down in the new state, which became a part of the Union in 1850. Still others, who had made their fortunes serving the needs of the miners, became leaders of industry. These businesses employed the thousands of people who had no jobs when the gold rush was over.

But wherever they went and whatever they became, the forty-niners would never forget the part they played in American history; an episode that seemed more like fantasy than fact, more like a dream than real life.

# THE DRAMA UNFOLDS

**IT COULD BE SAID** that the story of the gold rush really began on the day in 1839 when John Augustus Sutter first arrived in California. He brought little with him from Switzerland except his dream of creating a farming empire in this sleepy possession of Mexico. Mexico had broken away from Spanish rule in 1821 and claimed California for itself. Millions of acres in California that once belonged to Spain were now owned by Mexican officials. Thousands of cattle grazed and grew fat on these huge land grants. They became California's leading, and only, product. The time and place seemed to be perfect for making Sutter's dream come true.

Sutter applied for Mexican citizenship. In 1840 he received a land grant of nearly 50,000 acres (20,235 hectares), in the Sacramento Valley. He built a fort made of adobe near the south bank of the American River. From this fort, he controlled the surrounding land, which he named New Helvetia. (Helvetia is another name for Switzerland.)

Meanwhile, overland emigrants from the United States began to arrive in the valley. They had followed trails established by fur trappers. After 1841, this route through the midsection of the country became known as the California Trail.

Settlers in this period before the gold rush also came by ship. More than 200 Mormons came ashore at Yerba Buena (soon to be called San Francisco). They had sailed around Cape Horn, the southernmost tip of South America, hoping to escape from the religious persecution they had experienced in the East. Many of them found work at Sutter's Fort.

By January 1848, Sutter's Fort was a lively place with a population of nearly 300. More settlers arrived every day, and a sawmill was urgently needed. Sutter appointed a carpenter named James Wilson Marshall to supervise construction of a sawmill about 45 miles (72.4 km) east of the fort. The location was at a bend in the south fork of the American River in the Coloma Valley.

On the afternoon of January 14, Marshall walked along a ditch that channeled water from the river to the sawmill. Earlier, he thought he had seen some shiny pebbles in the ditch and wanted to examine them more closely. He picked

**Settlers had been traveling to California before the gold rush, but they really started to come in swarms after this precious metal was discovered.**

up a pebble about the size of a pea, and his heart began to race. It looked too yellow to be silver but didn't seem bright enough to be gold. He pounded it. It bent but didn't break. Could it be?

Marshall hurried back to some workmen, who were resting at the end of a long day. He announced that he had just found gold. At first, they were unimpressed. Only Henry Bigler, a Mormon from Virginia, thought it might be significant. In his diary, he wrote, "This day some kind of mettle [metal] was found in the tail race that looks like goald [gold]."

The next day, the workmen decided to have a better look at the shiny pebbles. Within minutes, they realized James Marshall knew what he was talking about. He really had discovered gold!

As news of James Marshall's gold discovery at the sawmill reached the Mormons at Sutter's mill, they, too, began to look for gold. They discovered enough to abandon their regular work and begin mining in earnest. This second site became known as Mormon Island.

After Marshall told Sutter of his discovery, Sutter tested the pebbles for himself and became convinced they were gold. He established legal claim to the land, buying it directly from the Indians. Then he asked his workers to say nothing of the discovery for six weeks. But even Sutter himself could not keep quiet. He wrote to his friend, Mar-

Sutter's Mill, in the Coloma Valley, where James Marshall discovered gold, and where a nation was changed forever iano Vallejo, less than a week later, saying that he had discovered a "mina de oro."

By the second week of March, news of the discovery reached San Francisco. It traveled by word of mouth until the fifteenth, when the news appeared in print for the first time. However, the story appeared on the last page of the San Francisco *Californian* and was only one paragraph long. Even a second story in the other weekly newspaper, the *California Star*, did little to interest the local folks.

The owner of the *Star* was an enterprising man named Sam Brannan. He decided to put out a special edition and send it to the folks in the eastern United States. With this edition, he hoped to persuade people to move to San Francisco and buy the lots he owned. Then he would make a profit for himself.

San Francisco citizens remained skeptical about the gold discovery. But ranchers near Sutter's Fort began to believe it after they saw the results of the Mormon diggings at a flour mill site. They came and staked out claims for themselves.

Sam Brannan arrived next. After he saw that workers at Sutter's Fort were in a frenzy over the discovery, he bought up future store locations. Those who already had been prospecting displayed their pouches of gold dust as they prepared to dig for more. Sam Brannan realized that something important had happened here. He was determined to be a part of it.

**Exaggerated stories about the West were always coming East. At first, average citizens did not believe the gold rush was real. Even valid newspaper articles did not inspire the masses to travel to California.**

These men happily announce their discovery of gold.

On May 12, Brannan returned to San Francisco, displaying a bottle full of gold dust and shouting, "Gold! Gold! Gold from the American River." Excited people gathered around to ask questions and wonder. But they didn't wonder long. On May 12, there were six hundred men in the city. Three days later, there were two hundred. The others had gone to the gold field. By the end of the month, the city had nearly closed down. Even the newspapers ceased operation—there was no one left to read them. Soon, men from all over California left other jobs and headed for the hills.

Two thousand copies of Sam Brannan's special edition *Star* reached Missouri by the end of July. Many newspapers reprinted stories from it, but most people dismissed the gold discovery idea. It was unimportant, they said, or too good to be true. So, they ignored it.

But the news wouldn't die. Stories continued to trickle back East in letters by private citizens and reports from government officials. Throughout the summer and fall, newspapers featured more stories about the great wealth to be found in the West. What most Americans needed, however, was official support for these tall tales. Finally, on December 5, 1848, President James K. Polk delivered a message to Congress. In it, he said that the news of California's gold discovery had been verified. Those tales weren't fiction; they were fact!

The gold rush was on!

**AS NEWS OF GOLD** continued to travel east, men of every age and occupation made plans to go to California. The New York *Herald* reported, "All classes of our citizens seem to be under the influence of this extraordinary mania. . . ."

But how should they plan to travel? There was no easy way. California was so far away that it would take months to reach the gold fields, and at great expense. Speed was something to consider in choosing a route, and so was cost. Danger was another factor to think about. Hardly anyone worried about comfort—yet.

Most of the forty-niners chose the type of transportation with which they were most familiar. Those who lived on farms or in small towns in the Midwest decided to travel overland by wagon. Many of them had traveled by wagon to reach their present homes. Moving farther west, using the same kind of transportation, would be nothing new.

Those who lived near the sea elected to go by ship. Many of these men earned their living as seamen or shipbuilders. Now, to go on the biggest adventure of their lives, it was natural to choose a water route. They had two from which to pick: around South America by way of Cape Horn or the Strait of Magellan, or a land-water route via the Isthmus of Panama, a narrow bridge of land joining North and South America. Less popular land-water routes crossed Nicaragua or Mexico to get from the Atlantic Ocean to the Pacific.

Those who were most eager to reach the gold fields chose to go by way of Panama. The route was shorter by months than traveling by either Cape Horn or overland. But it was also the most expensive way to go.

Typically, the voyage from New York City to Chagres, Panama, lasted about three weeks, including stops along the way to refuel and pick up more passengers. After the gold seekers landed, they rented long canoes, called *bungos*, for a three-day trip on the Chagres River through thick, steamy jungle. About 40 miles (64 km) upriver, the travelers came to a village named Cruces, where they transferred to mules for the rest of the trip to Panama City, 20 miles (32 km) away.

The sights and sounds across the Isthmus were new to most of these travelers. At first, the brightly colored birds

**The steamer *Hartford*, leaving New York City, was filled with Argonauts bound for California.**

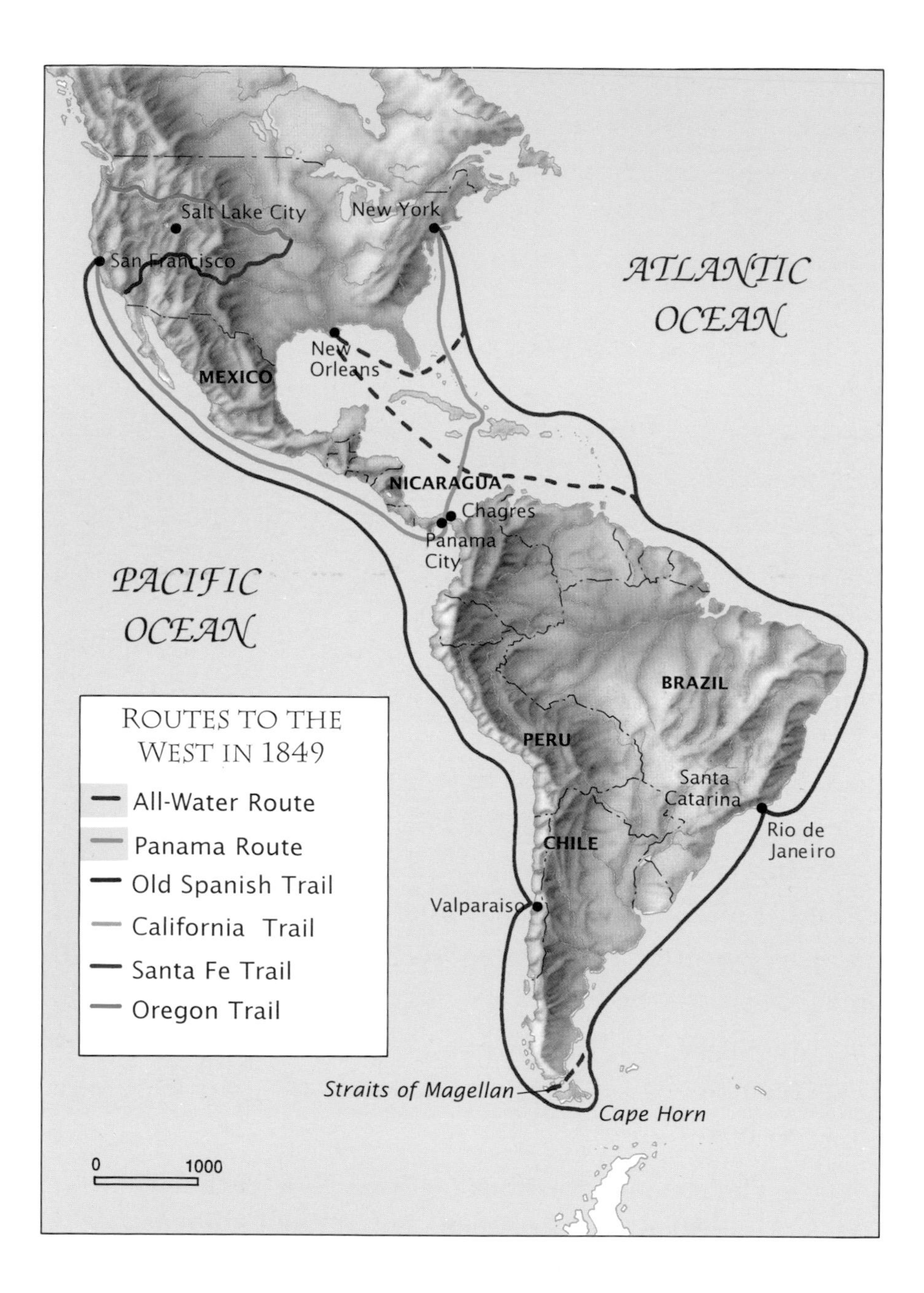
Salt Lake City
New York
San Francisco
ATLANTIC OCEAN
New Orleans
MEXICO
NICARAGUA
Chagres
Panama City
PACIFIC OCEAN
BRAZIL
PERU
Santa Catarina
Rio de Janeiro
CHILE
Valparaiso
Straits of Magellan
Cape Horn
ROUTES TO THE WEST IN 1849
All-Water Route
Panama Route
Old Spanish Trail
California Trail
Santa Fe Trail
Oregon Trail
0
1000

and noisy, strange-looking animals were a novelty. The poisonous snakes, however, were frightening. Most irritating were the armies of insects that marched over them day and night. The daily downpour of rain left everything soggy and unfit to use, and this, too, did not help the forty-niners' outlook.

The tropical fruit was good, and there was plenty of water. But everything was contaminated. With the bad food, water, and insects came diseases such as yellow fever, malaria, and cholera. Everyone caught something.

For one traveler, the discomfort outweighed everything else. He wrote: "First, stay home. Second, if you go to California, take any route but this."

Once the forty-niners arrived at Panama City, they often had to wait for days or weeks for a ship to take them the rest of the way. When it finally arrived, there was little room to take on more passengers because the boat already had twice as many as it was built to carry.

Arguments arose, and fights broke out among those who waited. Finally, more people were crowded on board, and many of the ships "were filled to crammation," as one ship captain expressed it. Although the trip from Panama City to San Francisco was the shortest part of the journey, it must have seemed like an eternity to those on board who were eager to begin mining.

For the 15,000 people who traveled around Cape Horn or through the Strait of Magellan in 1849, an eternity didn't

begin to describe the length of their trip. Lasting from four to nine months, the sea voyage of 18,000 miles (28,800 km) began in Atlantic or Gulf ports of the United States. It then followed the east coast of South America and rounded the dangerous cape or sailed through the strait before turning north. The trip ended at San Francisco, after a long, tortuous crawl along the coast of South and North America.

The emigrants on these ships, called *Argonauts* after the gold seekers in Greek mythology, knew about the dangers on this route. Terrifying storms with mountainous seas and gale-force winds seemed to blow in from out of nowhere. Navigators had none of the early-warning devices we have today. Shipwrecks were not uncommon. Navigating the strait was a somewhat shorter trip, but its currents and rugged shoreline made some Argonauts regret this choice of passage.

There were other hazards on board. Fires spread quickly from unruly cookstoves and food soon spoiled due to lack of refrigeration. Not many passengers felt like eating at the beginning of the trip anyway. Seasickness was common and, without modern-day medicines, little could be done to relieve it. Living quarters were filthy, overcrowded, and unsanitary.

Perhaps one of the worst problems was boredom. Some passengers organized card games, and some performed dramas or musicales (musical variety shows). If educated men were among the passengers, they preached on Sun-

**This advertisement for the *Eagle Wing* clipper ship says it will reach San Francisco in 106 or 117 days—if passengers were lucky—but that could never be guaranteed.**

**These forty-niners follow the trail over a mountain range on their way to California.**

days, lectured on science, and printed a weekly news sheet. Everyone who could write kept journals and wrote letters home to be posted once they docked.

The boredom was interrupted by several stops along the way. On the Atlantic side, ships usually anchored at Rio de Janeiro or Santa Catarina in Brazil. There, the Argonauts could go ashore, eat decent food, drink safe water, and catch up on news from the States. Once around the Horn or

through the strait, the ships usually stopped again at Valparaiso, Chile, to make repairs and buy more supplies for the last part of the journey.

The most popular way to go west was overland. Although figures are not reliable, some historians think about 40,000 emigrants used the two main overland routes to California in 1849.

Much planning took place before the trip began. Wagons and livestock had to be strengthened for the long, hard journey. Covered wagons would be used as a home for many months. Familiar belongings, such as quilts, dishes,

chairs, stoves, trunks, and even musical instruments were carried along. Later, these comforts would help the settlers establish new homes in California. More women and children traveled west this way than by any other route.

Most of the emigrants organized themselves into groups, or companies, before they departed. Usually, these companies were made up of families, friends, and neighbors. These people could be counted on for companionship and help if the need arose. The travelers also felt there was safety in numbers. Emigrants had heard about Indian hostility and wanted to be prepared. Some caravans became so large they stretched for several miles along the trail.

As it happened, 1849 turned out to be a very wet year. To the emigrants, as they gathered at the trailheads in April, rain meant long, lush prairie grass, which would provide abundant food for their livestock along the way. In their excitement, they forget that rain also made trails muddy and creeks too high to cross. Finally, rain or no rain, the wagon trains could wait no longer. At the end of the month they set off on their trip.

The Santa Fe Trail wound its way through southern territory won in the Mexican War. However, the best-known and most popular was the California Trail. The four- to six-month trip began in Missouri or Iowa. Then it veered northwest along the Platte River to Fort Kearney in the Nebraska territory and Fort Laramie in what is now Wyoming. The first weeks were the easiest, unless it rained.

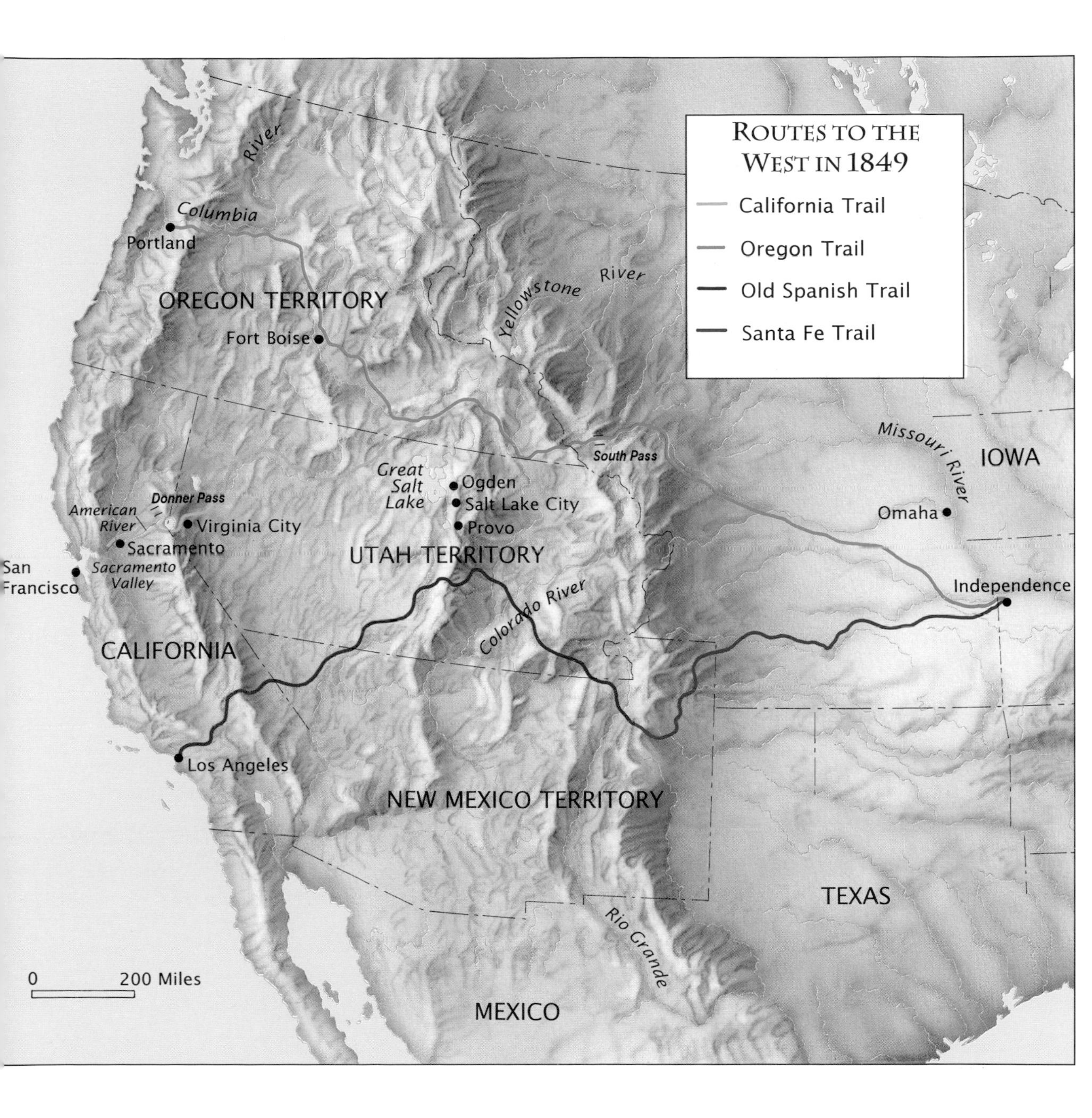

Routes to the West in 1849
California Trail
Oregon Trail
Old Spanish Trail
Santa Fe Trail
Columbia River
Portland
OREGON TERRITORY
Fort Boise
Yellowstone River
South Pass
Missouri River
IOWA
Omaha
Great Salt Lake
Ogden
Salt Lake City
Provo
Donner Pass
American River
Virginia City
Sacramento
San Francisco
Sacramento Valley
UTAH TERRITORY
Independence
Colorado River
CALIFORNIA
Los Angeles
NEW MEXICO TERRITORY
TEXAS
Rio Grande
MEXICO
0
200 Miles

Humans and animals alike were weary by the time they reached their destination.

As the trail stretched out flat and straight to the horizon, the emigrants fought boredom rather than Indians, who turned out not to be so hostile after all. The beauty and wonders of the trail interrupted the boredom now and then, as the emigrants marveled at outcroppings called Chimney Rock, Courthouse Rock, Castle Bluffs, and Scotts Bluff. Wild game and wild flowers were other beauties of nature they enjoyed as they traveled west.

Following the Sweetwater River in what is now Wyoming, the trail gradually climbed to South Pass. There, forty-niners could choose to go north on the Oregon Trail, or south. Most of them went south to the Mormons' newly established settlement at Great Salt Lake. As spring turned into summer and the flatland became rocky, mountainous terrain, the trail grew more treacherous. Wagon breakdowns were common, and time was lost in trying to repair them. Wagons were often left by the side of the trail, along with precious family possessions.

From Great Salt Lake, the travelers followed the Humboldt River to the Humboldt Sink through the Forty-Mile Desert. Water became more difficult to find, the dust harder to swallow, and the intense heat a struggle to survive.

Crossing the Sierra Nevada range was the final challenge. Sometimes early freezes brought bitter cold before the emigrants finally dipped down into the Sacramento Valley and neared their final destinations. For these weary travelers, however, one adventure had just ended and another was about to begin.

**SHIPLOADS OF FORTY-NINERS** began arriving in California by the early summer of 1849. They landed at San Francisco, once a sleepy village of less than 900 residents. Now, it had been awakened by thousands of adventurers from all over the world. They stayed only long enough to outfit themselves and find transportation to the "diggings."

The village grew quickly to accommodate the Argonauts. It sprawled along the docks in a collection of wooden huts and tents. Its harbor was crowded with ships abandoned by owners who had gone to the gold fields. Living conditions were crowded and expensive. A small room rented for $50 a month, ten times what it cost in the East. Wood was so expensive that one man paid $100 for a small packing box—to live in!

Even though there was no gold to be discovered in San Francisco, it went from a village to a crowded city practically overnight, as travelers passed through on the way to seek their fortunes.

Some of the newcomers quickly realized that all of the gold wasn't to be found in the hills. They stayed in San Francisco, opening businesses which catered to the needs of the miners. They charged $10 for a hat, $100 for a pair of boots, $100 for a blanket, and $50 for a shovel. The new merchants soon prospered, and so did the village. By 1850, it had grown to a city of 56,000.

The prospectors used any kind of transportation they could afford to get to the mines. Some traveled by riverboat to Sacramento or Stockton. Others journeyed by horse, mule, or foot. Those who arrived via the California Trail had a head start. They hardly paused in Sacramento before pushing on to the gold fields.

At first, everyone wanted to go to the Coloma Valley. Soon, however, mining camps popped up all along the curves of the Sierra foothills. The banks of the American, Feather, and Yuba rivers became populated with settlements as well. Wherever gold was discovered, a camp was soon established. Many of them were given funny, colorful names, such as Bedbug, Total Wreck, and Ten-Cent Gulch.

Prices soared at the tent stores in the diggings. But the miners either had to pay them or go without supplies. A slice of bread cost a dollar, and it took another dollar to butter it. An egg cost from one to three dollars. Nearly all the other basics—flour, sugar, and coffee—sold at ridiculous prices *when* they were available.

The reason was not hard to understand. Local farmers and ranchers had raced off to become miners. They left their crops to die, and no one bothered to replant. Now, food had to be shipped great distances, driving prices nearly out of reach. Since actual money was scarce, gold dust soon became the currency of exchange. A pinch of dust (the amount anyone could pick up between his thumb and forefinger) was supposed to equal one dollar.

Life was simple, though far from easy, in the mining settlements. The miners rose at dawn, emerging from crudely made shacks, tents, or blankets laid on bare ground under the trees. The weather could be cold and wet at times, and blizzards were not uncommon in the winter. There was no plumbing. The miners bathed in streams. They cooked breakfast over an open fire. Salt pork and bread usually made up both their morning and evening meals. Coffee washed everything down, when they could get it. A real treat, saved for special occasions such as Christmas, was a can of peaches.

Because of their unhealthy diets and harsh living conditions, miners suffered from many ailments. Fevers, chills, and rheumatism were common complaints after weeks of working in icy streams. Scurvy, dysentery, and diarrhea were other discomforts caused by poor diets and food eaten half-raw or spoiled. One miner complained that the bread he bought was full of worms. Even with gold dust in his pockets, however, he could find no decent bread to buy.

# GOOD NEWS

FOR

# MINERS.

## NEW GOODS,

## PROVISIONS, TOOLS,

## CLOTHING, &c. &c.

## GREAT BARGAINS!

JUST RECEIVED BY THE SUBSCRIBERS, AT THE LARGE TENT ON THE HILL,

A superior Lot of New, Valuable and most DESIRABLE GOODS for Miners and for residents also. Among them are the following:

### STAPLE PROVISIONS AND STORES.

Pork, Flour, Bread, Beef, Hams, Mackerel, Sugar, Molasses, Coffee, Teas, Butter & Cheese, Pickles, Beans, Peas, Rice, Chocolate, Spices, Salt, Soap, Vinegar, &c.

### EXTRA PROVISIONS AND STORES.

Every variety of Preserved Meats and Vegetables and Fruits, [more than eighty different kinds]. Tongues and Sounds; Smoked Halibut; [illegible] Fish; Eggs [illegible], Figs, Raisins, [illegible]; China Preserves; China Bread and Cakes; Butter Crackers, Boston Crackers and many other very desirable and *choice bits*.

### DESIRABLE GOODS FOR COMFORT AND HEALTH.

Patent Cot Bedsteads, Mattresses and Pillows, Blankets and Comforters. Also, in Clothing—Overcoats, Jackets, Miner's heavy Velvet Coats and Pantaloons, Woolen Pants, Guernsey Frocks, Flannel Shirts and Drawers, Stockings and Socks, Boots, Shoes; Rubber Waders, Coats, Blankets, &c.

### MINING TOOLS, &c.; BUILDING MATERIALS, &c.

Cradles, Shovels, Spades, Hoes, Picks, Axes, Hatchets, Hammers; every variety of Workman's Tools, Nails, Screws, Brads, &c.

### SUPERIOR GOLD SCALES. MEDICINE CHESTS, &c.

Superior Medicine Chests, well assorted, together with the principal Important Medicines for Dysentery, Fever and Fever and Ague, Scurvy, &c.

### N.B.—Important Express Arrangement for Miners.

The Subscribers will run an EXPRESS to and from every Steamer, carrying and returning Letters for the Post Office and Expresses to the States. Also, conveying "*GOLD DUST*" or Parcels, to and from the Mines to the Banking Houses, or the several Expresses for the States, insuring their safety.——The various *NEWSPAPERS* from the Eastern, Western and Southern States, will also be found on sale at our stores, together with a large stock of *BOOKS* and *PAMPHLETS* constantly on hand.

Excelsior Tent, Mormon Island,
January 1, 1850.

ALTA CALIFORNIA PRESS

WARREN & CO.

From Original

Courtesy of Bancroft Library

148. Mormon Island Emporium, Excelsior Tent

**Even though this advertisement promised "great bargains," miners often paid more for supplies than what we would pay at today's prices!**

Doctors, or men who called themselves that, posted signs reading "Hospital" across their tents and waited for patients to arrive. The only medical weapons against disease at that time were painkilling drugs. Quinine, which could ease malaria, cost four times its weight in gold. It's easy to understand why one out of five miners died in the first year of the gold rush. It's more difficult to understand how so many others survived!

In the evenings, miners sat around their campfires and told stories of home. Sometimes they played card games, but not for long. After a long, hard day of mining, they thought of little else but sleep.

The miners had chosen a backbreaking occupation. They worked alone at first, dressed in dark pants, red flannel shirts, and broad-brimmed hats. In the early days, they would stand knee-deep in icy streams, for ten or twelve hours a day, panning for gold.

Panning was the simplest and easiest way to separate gold from dirt. Gravel and water were mixed together in a pan or any other similar container. The pan was swirled around until the water washed the lighter dirt away. With luck, the heavier material left at the bottom of the pan was gold.

Miners soon began to use rockers, or cradles, to sift the dirt. A rocker was a rectangular box, mounted on rockers (like a rocking chair) and set on sloping ground. Cleats, wooden or metal spikes, were fastened to the bottom. Dirt

**Miners had great hope that the next pan would yield the nugget of gold that would make them rich.**

"Cradling" for gold enabled miners to wash through more dirt than panning did, and was even more efficient when two miners worked together.

was put in the top, and water was added to send the dirt through the box. The heavier gold fell to the bottom, catching on the cleats. More dirt could be washed with a rocker than with a pan. But the individual miner really needed a partner to make the process more efficient.

Other methods of mining were invented as the supply of placer, or surface, gold dwindled. Sluice boxes—used to wash out the gold—were larger versions of rockers, requiring many miners working together. Later, hydraulic mining came into use. It turned out to be the most efficient method, but it was also the most destructive. Water, applied under great pressure to banks of gravel, caused the ground to disintegrate. Once the gold was taken from the gravel, the miners moved on, leaving ruined hillsides behind.

Eventually, dredging and quartz mining developed. These methods required more complicated tools, more money, and more miners working together. Gold mining then ceased to be an adventure and became a business.

Most miners rested on Sunday. That was the day they chopped wood for the following week's campfires, repaired their tools, and washed clothes in nearby streams. They also wrote letters to their families and put down their thoughts in journals. The gold rush was one of the most written-about events in United States history.

Sometimes a preacher rode through the territory, or was already at the camp as a miner. He preached for those willing to listen, although religion did not play a large part

**Hydraulic mining was a successful means of finding gold, but its effects on the land were disastrous. Those who used hydraulic mining left a trail of destruction behind them.**

**This oil painting entitled *Sunday Morning in the Mines* shows the varied tasks miners carried out on their day of rest: some read, some wrote, some washed, and some recovered from Saturday night's festivities.**

in miners' lives until their families joined them. Most miners considered a sermon as nothing more than a form of entertainment. And it was entertainment they missed most from their old lives.

Soon, they began to organize social events like the ones they had enjoyed at home. Men who could play a musical instrument were often called on to play tunes that everyone could sing. "Oh! Susannah" was a favorite, and so was "Wait for the Wagon" and "Camptown Races." Sometimes, dances were held. Since there were few women around, the men danced with one another.

Holidays were an excuse for major celebrations. The Fourth of July was a favorite occasion. If someone had an American flag, it was unfurled from a tree. If a flag wasn't available, someone made one from material on hand. Red calico always found its way into homemade flags in the early days of mining camps.

Parades were common on the Fourth. So, too, was anyone who could "speechify," or give a patriotic talk. The crude bars of the camps became crowded as the day went on. By nightfall, fights usually broke out among the rowdy, celebrating miners. This, too, was considered part of the entertainment.

Professional entertainers began to make appearances at the camps soon after they were established. The miners would pay well, in gold dust of course, to see them sing, dance, or act. Famous singers of the period began their careers in the camps, including Lola Montez and a young

A miner's ball. When the forty-niners let loose, they really had a good time.

girl named Lotta Crabtree. Lotta was only eight when she began her career, and soon became one of the most popular entertainers in the West. Miners walked miles to hear her sing.

Miners were generous with entertainers, and with one another as well. They helped if someone ran out of money or food or lost his tools. In the early days, everyone was honest, too, and there was no need for laws. Miners left their gold dust in their tents. No one stole it. If someone borrowed an ax or shovel, it was always returned.

But as the population grew, problems arose. The question of land ownership was one of the first. (Ownership by Indians didn't count under the settler's rules.) Miners soon worked out a system. They simply claimed, as their own, the land they had staked out for mining. The size of the claim varied from camp to camp. It might be as small as 10 square feet (3 sq m) or as large as 50 (15 sq m).

Ownership of that claim was established with the claim officer of the camp. A piece of personal property left at the site was another sign of ownership. A pick, shovel, hat, or shirt would do. If the claim was not worked within a certain time, however, it could be taken over by someone else.

As crime increased, more law and order was needed. When a law was broken, the miners quickly appointed an *alcalde*, or magistrate, to conduct a trial in a hastily assembled court. Miners came from miles around to attend the proceedings and also be part of the jury. Sometimes a flogging or lashing was considered punishment enough.

**Lola Montez was born in Ireland and was quite accomplished as a dancer before heading to the American West, where she was a great success.**

But justice could be extremely harsh. One mining camp became known as Hangtown after three men were quickly tried and found guilty—and just as quickly hanged from a tree on the main street of camp. Hangtown's reputation for hasty, hard justice helped to keep outlaws away. Soon, it no longer needed such a morbid name. In 1850, the legislature of the new state named the camp Placerville.

Prejudice against foreigners contributed to the increase of crime. Since more than one-fourth of the miners came from outside the United States, bigoted miners had many targets for their prejudice. Mexicans and Chileans arrived first, bringing with them a knowledge of mining and a willingness to work hard. Miners from the British Isles brought a belief in tommyknockers, elves believed to protect miners from harm. Political problems at home sent German and French miners to California, in search not only of gold, but also a better way of life.

The Chinese were slower in arriving. In 1850, they numbered 600 in the state. Indians, who were native to the area, were never even counted in any of the census reports and ranked lowest on the social scale in the mines.

At first, everyone seemed to work together. But, as more foreigners arrived, resentment grew. They were subjected to discrimination and harassment. On April 13, 1850, the California legislature decreed that every miner not from the United States needed to pay a tax of $20 a month. Many miners, foreign ones especially, hardly made that much.

**The various ethnic groups that sought gold in California are represented in this painting called *In Front of the Empire Saloon*.**

When they could no longer mine, they turned to other sources of income, many of them illegal.

In Sonora, a mining camp 60 miles (86.5 km) south of Coloma, resentment and rebellion against the Foreign Miners' Tax grew quickly. Violence erupted the first time taxes were levied. Sonora became an armed camp, and no one felt safe. Fights broke out, lives were threatened, and great numbers of Mexicans were imprisoned. It took months to restore order.

French miners also were disturbed by the tax since they, too, experienced unfair treatment in the gold fields. Near Mokelumne Hill, a group of Frenchmen had discovered a very rich claim. American miners soon tried to move in, but the French placed their own tricolored flag on it. Angry Americans gathered in force, rushed the claim, and carried away a fortune in gold. This act went unpunished and became known as the French War.

The Foreign Miners' Tax was repealed in 1851, but not before many had suffered needlessly. It was reenacted a year later, at $3 a month. By 1855, the tax was raised to $6, and the legislature provided funds to translate its terms into Chinese so the Chinese miners could read it. By then, the Chinese in California numbered over 25,000.

Ironically, many of the foreign miners stayed in California despite the prejudice against them. Eventually, they became citizens and made remarkable contributions to the state that had first tried to get rid of them.

# AFTER 1849

**THE PACE OF LIFE** hardly slowed at all after the first full year of the gold rush. Miners feverishly continued to dig, pan, sluice, and blast gold out of the hills and streams. When a vein was played out, they moved on, eager and restless to find another strike. On their rare days away from the diggings, the miners hurried to town. Now, they began to look for ways to save their gold rather than spend it. At the beginning of the rush, there were no banks in California. This was quickly corrected, and soon miners were able to exchange their dust and nuggets for coins and bills.

Gradually, miners settled in one mining camp. They built sturdier cabins, planted gardens, and sent for their families. Camps became towns with elected officials as miners became more concerned about real law and order.

Miners continue their search for gold.

Frontier justice, with its makeshift trials and speedy punishments, was a thing of the past.

In 1853, women still made up only 15 percent of the population. But their presence had a powerful effect on the rest of the inhabitants. Men bathed more often. They dressed better. There were fewer of them in gambling halls. Churches and schools were established, and children marched in parades that once saw only miners.

The gold rush had attracted many ambitious, intelligent men with a strong sense of adventure. Once the rush was over, they quickly pushed on with the rest of their lives. Some of them followed gold or silver strikes to Colorado, Nevada, or Australia. Others went home.

Those who stayed returned to their original occupations when their "get rich quick" schemes faded. Educators returned to teaching. Preachers became preachers again. Carpenters returned to building. Farmers turned to the land once more. By 1855, California was producing nearly all the food it consumed. This is remarkable considering that a few years earlier miners had died from scurvy due to lack of fresh fruits and vegetables.

Former businessmen opened retail stores, lumber mills, brickyards, iron foundries, and machine shops. They laid out railroads and began steamship lines. Some even began new careers as a result of their gold rush experiences.

Levi Strauss was a former peddler. In 1853, he went west to sell tent canvas to miners, but saw a need for sturdy pants. He stayed on to begin a successful wholesale clothing business in San Francisco, and today he is known as the inventor of Levi's blue jeans.

Mark Hopkins began his California career when he opened a grocery and hardware store in Sacramento in 1849. Later, with Collis Potter Huntington, Charles Crocker, and Leland Stanford, he financed the Central Pacific Railroad of California. It became California's link to the rest of the country and made its four founders far richer and more famous than any gold strike ever could.

Mark Hopkins's grocery store didn't sell meat, however. That was handled only by butchers, such as Philip Danforth Armour. Soon he was keeping miners up and down the gold highway supplied with meat. He made enough money to return to the East and begin a meat-packing business. Americans continue to buy Armour meat products today.

Another gold rush pioneer was John M. Studebaker, who came west to make wagons for the miners. After the rush, he returned to South Bend, Indiana. With $4,000 he had saved, he continued his wagon business on a grand scale. Those wagons were the forerunners of Studebaker automobiles, one of the country's most popular cars in the 1950s and 1960s.

Life after the gold rush was not as kind to James Wilson Marshall and John Augustus Sutter. Marshall prospected for a while, then moved on to other jobs with no future and little pay. After the state legislature voted a $200-a-month

**California was granted statehood soon after gold was discovered. Although it had to import most of its food during the gold rush, California quickly became an agricultural giant.**

pension for him, he spent most of it on liquor. When he died in 1885, he was penniless and alone.

Sutter lost everything he owned in California. In 1870, he moved to Pennsylvania and applied for federal aid several times. He, too, had no money. After his appeals were denied, he lived out the rest of his life in poverty. He died in 1880.

The gold rush was kindest of all to California. Gold gave the state a head start, making it famous overnight. Everyone wanted to go there, making transportation popular and profitable. Other industries sought out its favorable climate. Eventually, oil, agriculture, cattle, tourism, real estate, and the motion picture business outshone gold mining. But gold turned those dreams into reality. Gold is what brought California and its destiny of greatness together. In a way, the gold rush has never ended.

**Adobe**—sun-dried brick, made of clay.

**Alcalde**—Spanish word meaning "mayor" or "chairman" or "magistrate"; someone who has authority to serve as a judge.

**Argonauts**—a group of mythological heroes who traveled by ship in search of treasure. The forty-niners who traveled by ship to California were named for them.

**Bigoted**—having feelings of hatred or dislike against a race or religion not one's own.

**Bungos**—twenty-five-foot-long canoes used by natives of Panama.

**Cholera**—infectious disease, sometimes fatal. Patient suffers from vomiting and diarrhea.

**Civil War**—war that lasted from 1861 to 1865 between Northern and Southern states, and ended slavery.

**Cleats**—pieces of wood or metal projecting from sides and bottom of rocker, or cradle. Used to sift gold from dirt and debris.

**Diarrhea**—intestinal disorder.

**Dysentery**—intestinal disease characterized by severe diarrhea.

**Emigrants**—people who leave a country, or an area of it, to settle elsewhere.

**Eternity**—endless period of time; forever.

**Magistrate**—a person charged with carrying out the law.

**Malaria**—disease caused by a parasite carried by a mosquito. Patient suffers from chills and sweating.

**Migrate**—to go from one country, or an area of it, to another.

**Mormons**—another name for members of Church of Jesus Christ of Latter-Day Saints, begun in the United States in 1830.

**Ore**—metal-bearing mineral or rock.

**Overland**—travel across land rather than by sea.

**Persecution**—unfair treatment or attack on someone whose race or religion is different from one's own.

**Placer gold**—gold found on surface of earth. Miners did not have to dig to find it.

**Quinine**—medicine to treat malaria.

**Rheumatism**—physical ailment. Patient suffers from stiffness and pain in joints and back.

**Scurvy**—disease marked by swollen and bleeding gums due to lack of vitamin C in patient's diet.

**Sluice**—long, sloping trough for washing ores, and a method of washing ores or separating gold from dirt and debris.

**Trailhead**—where a trail begins.

**Veins**—lines of rocks containing mineral deposits.

**Yellow fever**—infectious disease carried by mosquitoes, usually occurring in hot, steamy climates.

# FOR FURTHER READING


Collins, James L. *Exploring the American West.* New York: Franklin Watts, 1989.

Lyngheim, Linda. *Gold Rush Adventure.* Van Nuys, CA: Langtry Publications, 1988.

McCall, Edith. *Gold Rush Adventures.* Chicago: Children's Press, 1980.

McNeer, May. *The California Gold Rush.* New York: Random House, 1962.

Stein, R. Conrad. *The Story of the Gold at Sutter's Mill.* Chicago: Children's Press, 1981.

# INDEX

# ABOUT THE AUTHOR

**ELIZABETH VAN STEENWYK** is the author of 40 books for young people and more than 150 articles for adult and children's magazines. She is the recipient of the Helen Keating Ott award for her outstanding contribution to children's literature, presented by the Church and Synagogue Library Association for 1990.

Mrs. Van Steenwyk lives in California. This is her first book for Franklin Watts.